HOTEL HORRORS & *HALOS...*

And Other Unforgettable Hospitality Moments

—BOOK TWO—

A MEMOIR BY
Jeannine Connor Gittens

Edited by Lil Barcaski

Published by: GWN Publishing
www.GWNPublishing.com

Cover Design: Kristina Conatser Captured by KC Design

ISBN: 978-1-959608-19-6

DEDICATION

This book is dedicated to my mom and my husband—two of the brightest lights on earth. One guiding me through the first half of my life with integrity, values, and unwavering love, and the other being my steadfast partner, love compass and best friend on life's very interesting journey over the past two decades.

Mommy, you're the best of them all. You never let life's many, MANY storms and challenges darken your heart. As your nieces and nephews always say, "Aunty is an angel walking the earth." Somehow always managing to keep a smile and a hearty laugh, your unwavering faith has been, and continues to be, inspirational. My own deep faith is now what I turn to when things seem gray. Thank you for every sacrifice you've ever made! I love you.

To my South American Prince Charming... Babe, there are no words to describe the love, respect, and admiration I have for you. From being the silly household comedian (guess that's where the boys get it from), to the astute and skillful businessman and BEST father, you're everything I didn't know I needed. Your love, patience, thoughtfulness, discipline, wit, and sheer brilliance has captained our family successfully with grace. Your constant encouragement and support made this book, and so many of my accomplishments, possible.

Thank you for everything, my love.

Cheers to quarter of a century down and forever to go!

CONTENTS

INTRODUCTION 2.0

Hey there... I'm Jeannine, just a gal from St. Croix, US Virgin Islands. Welcome to the second of two books about my hospitality career journey and some of the unique experiences I've had during two decades and several area codes. I've always been intrigued with the fine art of travel and meeting new people from all around the world.

My years enduring a tumultuous and highly dysfunctional childhood were spent hoping that one day I would escape the insanity. Addicted to reading, I was often scolded by my elementary school librarian, who threatened not to allow me to check-out more than 10 books at a time. (Yes, I said 10.) But there was something surreal in those pages. I loved reading about faraway places and learning about different cultures, customs, and languages.

As a pre-teen, the desire to see these places and meet diverse people tugged at my heartstrings and never let go. In Book 1, I share my story of how I went from being a Spanish major with high hopes, who volunteered at an airline to gain experience, to becoming the general manager at a renowned five-star celebrity haven.

When asked who my target audience is for these two books, I am quick to answer, "Everyone!" Honestly speaking, I do hope to inspire and educate those who want to succeed in this industry and are curious to know what it's REALLY like. I also want to put a smile to the face of the avid traveler who will recognize some of the personalities on these pages (hopefully, they're not the ones on the naughty list!). And of course, to my fellow hardworking, dedicated industry professionals, this is way to shed some light on the experiences we've collectively endured in one way or another.

My alphabetically designed memoir is full of deeply personal reflections and food for thought. I do hope you enjoy reading it as much I enjoyed writing it. Whether my memories make you chuckle, gasp, cringe or bust out in a knee-slapping belly laugh, I'm glad you're along for the ride. So, buckle up and let's get to it!

(And don't forget to grab a copy of Book 1 – with Chapters A to M - if you haven't done so already!)

—N—

NAKED & NEUROTIC
FROM NEW YORK

There's something very special about New York
City. Everyone on the planet knows that. It's one
of my favorite locations on earth. There's also
something unique about New Yorkers—and everyone in
hospitality knows that, too. I've met thousands of people
from the "Big Apple." Most were friendly, outgoing and
tons of fun. Others were notoriously rude, crass, and dis-
respectful. But a few were just downright freaky. This is
the story of an encounter with the latter...

A family of five arrived in a taxi. As they pulled up to
their private villa, three children approximately ages
five, seven, and nine jumped out of the sleek black van
and started running around wildly and screaming at
one another. After a day of travel, we assumed they were
just happy to release all that pent-up energy.

The waif-like mom/wife climbed out of the taxi next.
Her demeanor was clearly one of nonchalance border-

ing on indifference to what was happening. She never addressed the children, nor did she attempt to calm them down.

The dad/husband was the last to exit the vehicle. He stood there for a second, scowling at our pleasantly welcoming faces, then shoved past us to get into the front door of the villa. The rest of the family followed his lead.

Shocked into silence for a few heartbeats, I followed dutifully behind them and proceeded to launch into my welcome spiel. I presented the registration form for the man to sign while the rest of the staff busied themselves with bringing in the luggage, which amounted to just two suitcases, and then proceeded to serve the family canapes and drinks.

The first attitude bomb went off when Mr. Nutso started scratching out parts of our standard registration form, saying, "I'm a lawyer. I don't agree to this. And why shouldn't anyone be held accountable—what if the private chef decides to slit my child's throat in cold blood? Is that gonna be acceptable?" I heard an audible gasp from our executive chef who began to pray in Spanish while making the sign of the cross. Almost simultaneously, the three young children ran past us... naked... and dove into the pool by themselves. The husband looked up and yelled for his wife. She sauntered into the living room and walked right past him.

"Why the hell are they naked? Where's their swimsuits?" he asked.

She twirled around and, with a blank expression on her face, told him that she didn't know where their swimsuits were. She informed him that it seemed as though the kids had forgotten their suitcases back in New York.

Attitude bomb number two detonated right then and there. I could see that the staff wanted to run for cover. It felt surreal. His beet red face matched his manic screaming as the ballistic tirade continued. Fists tightly clenched at his side, he fumed and cursed his wife. She stood staring at him like she was completely bored. Keep in mind, all of this happened within the first ten minutes of the family's arrival. I expected a hidden camera reveal because crap like this was strictly for television.

Trying to stop the insanity playing out before me, I interrupted the chaos by suggesting that the guests visit one of the neighboring larger resorts where children's clothing would be available at their boutiques. I also advised that there were excellent local stores a bit further away but with more options. The wife looked at me, with a smirk on her face, and pointed to her husband. She said, "He can go get them new clothes. Call him a taxi." Then she twirled away, martini in hand, and sauntered out to the pool.

I immediately did as she requested, calling for a cab from my cell phone. The sputtering husband threw up his hands in despair and marched outside, resigned to wait for the taxi. I asked him if he preferred the resort route or if he wanted to go to the local children's boutiques. He didn't answer. I shrugged, told him the taxi would arrive in five minutes and went back to my office. I knew the villa staff would handle the situation with grace and professionalism as they continued with the orientation protocols. I thought, or at least prayed that, the worst of it was over.

It wasn't even 20 minutes later when my direct phone line started buzzing. The call was coming from "Villa Mayhem." I answered, timidly. After listening to the butler's fevered pleas for a few seconds, I bolted out of my chair and literally ran back to the villa. When I got inside, I gasped and blinked repeatedly. I could NOT believe my eyes. Standing atop the kitchen counter and, with precision that would have been better served in some sport, stood the redheaded, seven-year-old brat **PEEING IN THE SINK!** He wore the biggest grin of satisfaction on his little face.

I looked to the left and saw the staff's horrified and panicked faces. I looked to the right and saw Xanax-mom flipping through a magazine, thoroughly unbothered. Psycho-dad still hadn't returned from his impromptu shopping spree, and I had no idea where the other two children were.

In a split-second decision to go hard or go home, the "Caribbean mama" voice came out of my mouth. In the sternest possible tone, through clenched teeth, I walked up to the urinating child and hissed, "Now you listen here, young man. Get down from there IMMEDIATELY. In this country, we could call the police for something like this! Would you like me to call the police and tell them what you just did?"

His emerald eyes opened wide and he immediately jumped down with a thud running straight to his mom, wailing. But I didn't stop there; she was next in line for my professional tongue-lashing. I marched over to the mom and in a no-nonsense voice told her that what her son had done was unacceptable, unsanitary, and downright disgusting. I informed her that there would be a $250 sanitization fee added to their bill which would be charged immediately, given the gross situation and the urgency with which we would have to deal with it.

She looked up at me with the first real emotion I'd seen since she arrived. Her mouth fell open and she dramatically clutched her chest. I could see there was something snide about to roll off her tongue, but perhaps the look on my face made her think twice. Instead, she grabbed her son's hand, retreated to her master suite, and slammed the door.

I could literally hear the staff's collective sigh of relief to have them all out of sight for that moment. But as luck would have it, hubby rolled up just then. I breezed past him as he shuffled in the front door with several bags in his hand. Back in my office, I kept looking at the phone, expecting it to ring at any moment. It didn't. For the rest of the week, there were many other little fires that had to be put out with this family. So many fires, in fact, that when they checked out, they were the very first family name added to our now infamous DNA (DO NOT AC-CEPT) List. That list grew to about 15 names over the years. Some people are just not worth the headaches, no matter how much they're willing to pay.

—O—
OPULENT ORGIES

There are some things in this industry that you remember fondly. And there are things you wish you could permanently scrub from the recesses of your mind. This chapter is not for the faint of heart.

Once upon a time, I worked at an exquisite resort, renowned for its flamingo color, nestled in Palm Beach County, Florida. The extensive property was so large it sprawled city limits all the way to the beach. Celebs and the ultra-wealthy flocked to the massive hotel regularly. The service training was some of the best I've ever experienced. I incorporated much of what I'd learned there in my later years as an assistant manager and, ultimately, a general manager.

As part of the Guest Services management team, we would have special meetings when uber-elite guests were due to arrive. One morning, I walked into such a meeting and could not believe who our next VVIP guests would be. The only hint I'm willing to give is that this was a small group of men, linked to Emirati royalty of the most famous kind. I also knew I would probably never interact with these guests destined for the Presidential Penthouse and the adjacent luxury suites. I listened keenly to the agenda and noted the extreme security protocols that were being activated. The guests were only going to be in-house for three nights and four days, so I figured it would be a breeze. OH MAN, WAS I WRONG!

On the day the family checked out, all hell broke loose within the housekeeping department. Irate housekeepers were marching back and forth through the main hall, which was a rare sight. Actually, it was forbidden. Non-management staff members were to always remain "invisible" and were not allowed to walk through the public guest areas unless scheduled to work those specific areas.

Their shrill voices—many of them speaking rapid-fire Creole and Spanish—led me to believe something was terribly wrong. I exited my office and tried to cut off the line of men and women to ask what had happened to warrant such behavior. I grimaced as I listened to their very valid grievance. Apparently, the royals had left the resort's most coveted suites in a gruesome mess. Not your average stale-food-and-broken-bottles-of-booze kind of mess. It was all that, and then some.

Allegedly, the guests had called in some ladies (and men) to join them in their suites for down and dirty erotic services. The housekeepers reported that there was urine on the carpets, semen on the walls and sheets, drops of blood all over the marble floors and feces on the bathroom floors. The housekeepers said they'd rather quit than be made to clean up after those "nasty, filthy pigs."

Speechless and horrified, I went to my General Manager and reported what I had been told. The fact that he didn't even flinch let me know that he'd already gotten wind of the debacle. He managed a stressed smile and told me he was handling it. I walked out of his office and went back to my own.

Eventually, the senior management team offered the housekeeping staff three times their hourly wage—plus hazmat suits and a cash bonus—if they chose to clean the suites. Management also called in a professional sanitizing company to restore the suites to their pristine condition. I kept waiting for that story to show up on the local news, but thankfully, it never did. That would have been a royal mess!

If you've ever been on a group trip with friends, you know how exciting—and tedious—they can be. There is so much that goes into planning the perfect family reunion, girlfriend getaway or mancation. Whether it's choosing the location, coordinating the flights, or getting a consensus on the activities, it takes work! Sometimes, however, there are trips that color outside the lines of group travel norms. One such group hailed from Canada.

The group of four men and five women in their 50s arrived with chipper attitudes and a penchant for partying. From our prearrival contact with them, we knew that most of them were doctors and they religiously took an annual group vacation to "reset and reconnect." Having arrived by private jet late in the afternoon, they'd brought their own stash of premium liquor and exquisite delights such as caviar, filet mignon, and foie gras.

The leader of the group, who I'll call Abby, stated that they were a very private, fun-loving bunch who enjoyed catering to each other's needs. She went on to say that she would request housekeeping and other services when needed. Wasting no time, right after giving the chef their dinner preferences, they sent the remaining house staff away. I worked late that night, and when I left the premises close to 9 p.m., I could hear the blaring music and rowdy laughter that emanated from their villa. I thought to myself, "well they're really rocking out down there!"

The next day, the staff were re-directed to other guests because our "party animal" doctors had locked all the doors and posted a note outside saying, "No staff today." I would have thought an email could suffice, but hey, it was their choice.

All day long, we heard music and lots of hootin' and hollerin' coming from the house. Thankfully, no one was staying at the adjacent villa during their stay. The days flew by and I'd only heard the whispered rumors about the kinky group from Canada. They checked out late one evening. I had already bid them farewell earlier that afternoon.

When I got to my office the following morning, I opened the door and my mouth fell open immediately. Sitting in my chair was a huge inflated female sex doll in all her plastic glory, an envelope taped to her chest with my name on it. Shocked and wildly disturbed, I grabbed my phone and called the staff members who were onsite to come to my office urgently. One by one they filed in, stifling giggles.

When I asked if anyone could help me understand just what I was looking at, they burst out laughing and shared some hilarious facts with me. It seems as though my Canadian guests were quite the swingers. Per the housekeeping and dining service staff, they basically spent their entire vacation naked and having sex all over the villa, with and without toys, including sex dolls.

I didn't even know if I wanted to touch the envelope on the doll's body, let alone sit in my chair again until it was sanitized. I asked the bravest of the staff to get that doll out of my office while I pulled on some gloves to open the envelope. In it was a note from my esteemed guests, telling me how wonderful their stay was and that they wanted to rebook for the following year. And the clincher? They hoped they'd see more of me on the next trip because I had a secret admirer in the group.

I didn't know whether I should be flattered, scared, or nauseated. I was never one to judge what my guests did with their time and their money. I just didn't want to be a part of it. Ever. There we many other such guests and infamous stories that I cannot share, but these are the types of experiences that go hand in hand with this industry. You will literally "see it all!"

—P—

"PERKY TITS" AND PUPPY PROBLEMS

I t has been said that nothing can rekindle the dying flame of a relationship like a romantic getaway to the Caribbean. Idyllic, carefree days coupled with barefoot strolls along the beach after candlelit dinners can really do wonders for many. However, what happens when the very spot you so carefully selected for your "save-cation" becomes a nightmare for a weird reason?

The couple in this chapter was beautiful—inside and out. Both very friendly and charming, they acted like honeymooners. Mr. and Mrs. Ciccone shared that they had three young children back in Philly, all just barely a year apart in age, and were desperate to reconnect as husband and wife. They further divulged that they were hoping to "get their groove back," too. Why they'd decided to share all that info with me, a Guest Services Supervisor at the time, I have no idea. But I was happy that they were honest about what they wanted to accomplish on their vacation. Being heavily pregnant at the time myself, and in all my emotional feels, I wanted to help this couple in any way I could. I upgraded them to a beachfront suite at the most private end of the beach. I thought I was doing them a favor. (Insert *inner groan* here).

During the first three days of their stay, I only saw them twice. They looked happy and perfectly smitten with each other as they explored the boutiques and sipped cocktails at the General Manager's sunset happy hour. On the fourth day, disaster struck.

I glanced at the clock in the hotel lobby on that fateful afternoon. It was 3 p.m. In one glorious hour, I could go home, lie on my aching back, and put up my swollen feet while my husband gently massaged them. If I said my first pregnancy was rough, that would be a gross understatement. I vowed never to have another child once I'd safely delivered my firstborn. (Luckily, I eventually changed my mind on that.)

Starting on my end-of-shift paperwork in the back office, I made a mental note to check on the Ciccones the next day, which would be their last. Suddenly, I heard a male voice calling out, "Manager on duty! We need the manager on duty please." With a sigh, I knew that was my cue. Although only a supervisor, I was the only management level person on shift. I got up slowly, holding my huge belly, and limped to the front desk. Before me stood Mrs. Ciccone with a security guard. Her dark, wet hair clung to her tear-stained face. I immediately asked what happened.

Mrs. Ciccone began her monologue by saying, "I wanted to come to the Caribbean to fix my marriage. I came to this luxurious resort hoping that we could find our way back, but I was wrong. He is never going to change. Never! How can I compete with those sexy women? I've been breastfeeding for almost five years straight. I don't even have perky tits anymore. I thought nudity was illegal on this island... I checked before making the reservation. I don't need competition from toothpicks with perky tits, and now they're sitting outside my door on the beach!" She wiped away her tears, as her flushed face revealed her instant embarrassment and regret at having said those things aloud. I had no idea what she was talking about. In fact, unlike St. Martin, public nudity was not allowed on Anguilla. Were there naked people on the beach?

I glanced at the clock. It was 3:35 p.m. The cinnamon brown, 6'2", security guard shifted nervously and looked at me over the distraught woman's head as if to ask, "what the hell are we supposed to do about this?" I asked Mrs. C. where her husband was. Wrong question.

She exploded, "I just told you! He's sitting in our suite looking at those topless Italian bimbos with the perky tits! You need to get rid of them! They're ruining my marriage." She started sobbing loudly. New check-ins were starting to arrive, and I didn't want cause a bigger scene so I asked Mrs. Ciccone to show me where these alleged topless women were.

It was only then and there did I truly understand what she was saying. At the very end of the beach, where I'd tucked this couple for privacy, there were topless women sunbathing on the beach for her husband to behold. Now, as I waddled down the beach, sweating from head to toe, I realized this was all my fault. If I'd put them in a regular room and not upgraded them, I'd be on my way home, not struggling to walk down a beach in 90-degree heat to confront topless women. Ahhhh, the irony!

When we finally got to the location, there were indeed two strikingly beautiful women present with their bikini tops off. They were speaking to another security guard who was desperately trying to motion for them to cover their breasts. I glanced towards the Ciccone suite and saw Mr. C. trying to hide behind the blackout curtains, unsuccessfully, looking out at the commotion. His wife stood next to me with her hands on her hips, giving the women a fervent tongue-lashing they couldn't understand.

I tried to tell the women, in English, and using hand signs, that they needed to cover their breasts immediately and move from the area directly in front of the suite. They spoke to each other but didn't try to communicate with me or the two security guards. I spoke Spanish and knew that while both Spanish and Italian are Romance languages and very similar, they're still worlds apart.

Eventually, I rattled off a second warning in full Spanish, hoping it would make some semblance of sense to them, ending with I would call the 'policia' and pointed animatedly to the opposite end of the beach. That's when they stood up and started walking away, waving goodbye with a huge "Ciao" and blowing wind-kisses to the second security guard. I had to stifle a chuckle. By the way he was blushing, he was definitely sad to see them leave.

Eventually, Mr. Ciccone came out of the room, onto the beach, and tried to hug his wife. She wasn't having it. She pushed his arms away and trotted off down the beach, in the opposite direction of the two ladies. I never saw them again, but to this day, I think about that couple and wonder what happened when they got back to Philadelphia.

The joys of working in the airline industry will be forever etched in my soul. I was born to do it. It's in my DNA. While I enjoyed working in the islands for our regional puddle-jumper airlines, I was ecstatic to work at Miami International Airport for Cayman Airways.

The irony was not lost on me that of all the airlines I could have worked for in the USA, I got to work with a stellar company and still enjoy making Caribbean connections. The Caymanians were fun, feisty, and jovial. Also a highly regarded British Overseas Territory like Anguilla, I was familiar enough with their history and culture to feel right at home working with their team.

Still a college senior at the time, I only worked part-time, but my aim was to gain a full-time position by the time I graduated from FIU with my Spanish degree. Always willing to work overtime, I often made almost as much as a full-time employee anyway, so I figured I had a good chance of getting hired with benefits.

One wonderful Friday, a few days before Christmas, I was scheduled to work at 8 a.m. as I had no college classes. This was a busy day to work as we had passengers flying to not only Grand Cayman, but to Cayman Brac as well. This was also the day we had Cuban passengers, so I was always happy to practice my Spanish while checking in passengers.

The day ran smoothly, and when it was time for me to leave, my boss asked me if I could stay longer and work until the last flight around 8 p.m. I was already counting the overtime in my head! "Yes," was always my answer. After a filling Cuban lunch/early dinner of ropa vieja and a cortadito to keep me alert, I was ready to get those passengers checked in for the last flight.

The lines were long and messy. Christmas shoppers were in full-effect. Many passengers had multiple suitcases plus extra boxes and duffel bags. I earned my overtime for sure that evening.

Coming down to the last dozen or so passengers in line, I started to get really tired. I could feel it. The cortadito high was long gone. As my feet throbbed and my hands began to ache from lifting bags onto the belt, I just wanted it to be 8 p.m.

My next passenger, however, managed to give me a boost. A much older lady held a tiny cage with a glowing poodle inside. Such a cutie pie! We chatted about our holiday plans and the fact that on Cayman Brac, where she was headed, there were a few families with the last name Connor, like me. I checked her in, tagged her suitcases, and prepared the documents and tags for the animal separately. I bid her a safe flight and happy holidays.

After reconciling some info in the system, I looked up. And just like that, we'd finished processing the flight. There were no more passengers in line. Yippppeeee... It was time to wait for my supervisor, who drove me home most nights, and then go home to relax for the entire weekend.

Around 9:45 p.m. we received a call from Grand Cayman that there was a problem that had originated in Miami: a puppy was unclaimed and if no one came to get the animal, it could be put down. My heart started thumping so hard, I swore the entire room could see it. I vividly remembered checking in a puppy and chatting with my new "aunty." But could I have made an error in tagging the dog to the wrong island? Was I that tired? God, I really hoped not.

After getting the necessary info from the Customs officer in Grand Cayman, we traced the incident right back to who had checked in the animal. When my supervisor looked at me with a shocked expression on her face, I knew I was in the doghouse (pun most definitely intended!). Up until that point, I was a stellar employee. I was a naturally rising star in the company, loved by all—from the flight attendants to the ramp agents. Now, I thought, I'd singlehandedly screwed that up!

In her shrill Indian-British voice, my mentor lovingly chastised me for incorrectly tagging the puppy to Grand Cayman and not to the final destination of Cayman Brac. With hot tears springing forth and a deep fear in my heart, I apologized profusely. Disappointed in myself, I almost started to hyperventilate when I thought maybe I would lose my job over this... a job I loved with all my heart.

I was so dedicated to this airline that I would get a ride to work at 6:00 a.m. with my friend Patrick who worked at another airline, even though my shifts started at 8 or 9 a.m. I would walk around the terminals, greet other airline employees, stand in front of the Arrivals/Departures boards and marvel at all the flights. That's how much I loved working at the airport. I reveled in being amid the bustling, shuffling crowds, while hearing dozens of languages floating around me, coming from faces of every shade of skin.

At the thought of losing my job, I excused myself and went into the bathroom to bawl my eyes out. After a five-minute pity party, I splashed cold water on my face, went back to the main office and sat with my supervisor. Chin up and mentally resolved to fix this problem, I asked her what could I do to make this right. I asked if I could personally pay any fees or penalties to ensure the poodle would not be put down, or if I could pay for the puppy to be sent over to Cayman Brac that same night.

With a gentle pat on my hand, my beloved supervisor told me that it was all taken care of, and I should not worry. Shocked, I asked her a bucketload of questions. But she just smiled and said, "Please write up an incident report so that Mr. Sanchez will have it in the morning."

Yikes. I hadn't thought about that. Mr. Sanchez was the BIG boss. He was Mexican-American. and while friendly and carefree at times, he was first and foremost, a consummate professional. We got along well. He was equally amused and impressed by the fact that I had chosen to major in his native language. I hoped that the ounce of favor I'd always found with him would be worth its weight in gold after this particular incident.

I sat down and completed the formal incident report and then decided to write a personal letter to include in the packet. I explained in the letter to Mr. Sanchez that I took full responsibility for my actions and perhaps it was a wakeup call to not volunteer to work 12-hour shifts so much. I promised to be more attentive going forward and low-key begged not to be fired, but in a very non-begging kind of way.

And what can I say? Two days later, when I showed up for my shift, I was called into a meeting with Mr. Sanchez. He clasped his colossal hands as he sat behind his desk, looked me straight in the eye and said, "I admire what you did, and I appreciate the letter you wrote. That puppy could have met a very different fate, but thankfully, it all worked out. I will not issue a warning letter, but I must tell you, Jeannine, I hope that one day you will write a book. You're a very good writer."

Happy to know I was not going to be fired, I stood up and shook Mr. Sanchez's hand vigorously, beaming from ear to ear, and thanked him over and over for his graciousness. I have no idea where Mr. Sanchez is today, or if he is even alive, but I hope somehow, he will know that I've taken his advice... literally.

And as for my puppy problem? That little bundle of cuteness was reunited with his mama the very next morning. Merry Christmas it was indeed!

—Q—
QU'EST-CE QUE
C'EST??

My three-day elopement event in late January
1999 was perfect in every way. With our busy
work schedules and hundreds of relatives on
my side of the family alone, just the thought of planning
a wedding made me break out in hives. Because I am a
very private person, I wanted a calm, quiet, and no-flus-
ter type of affair. We told our parents what we planned
to do, and no one else. It felt a little naughty, but that was
part of the allure. We set a date and decided to get married on Dutch St. Maarten, enjoying an entire weekend
of European-Caribbean fun.

On the sunny, but unusually chilly, Sunday afternoon of
that weekend, we took a drive over to French St. Martin
to have lunch at Orient Bay. While I am fluent in Spanish, I loved the idea of getting a chance to practice my
only half-decent French when any opportunity arose.
While we were dressed for a typical beach day, I knew

that Orient Bay had a clothing optional policy and I mentally prepared myself for that. Or so I thought.

We drove our rental car to the beach and searched for parking. The beach was crowded and we drove in circles for almost 30 minutes, hoping someone would leave. Thankfully, just when we were about to abandon the idea of having lunch at this location, some local guys showed up and pointed us to a sliver of grass behind a sand dune where we could park our tiny car.

Stepping onto the main beach, we inhaled the salty air blended with the delectable scents of grilled meats and seafood. Walking along the wide stretch of sand was a journey in itself. In French St. Martin, the local creole food outlets are set up in side-by-side open warehouses known as lolos. Historically, this phenomenon evolved from the days of slavery and colonization. Even with a packed beach, there were many lolos to choose from, most with BBQ chicken or ribs, grilled lobster, whole snapper, and kebabs of all kinds.

As we strolled further towards the end of the beach with jumbo shrimp kebabs firmly in hand, I noticed many topless women sunbathing. Fully nude elderly folks and couples frolicked at the water's edge. It amazed me that the people you definitely didn't want to behold in the nude, often were the first ones to bare it all. Of course, I pretended I wasn't even looking when, in fact, I was seriously gawking behind my Ray Bans. I tried my best not to laugh out loud in some instances. Nevertheless, we strolled on, maneuvering through the "sand malls", insisting to the many vendors hawking their wares that we were fine and did not want to purchase any sarongs or get my hair braided. I was on a mission to find the stellar restaurant we'd heard so much about.

After a seven-minute walk, we entered the restaurant and sat at the bar. It was virtually empty. My husband-to-be went to the restroom after ordering a Ti' Punch. I began to peruse the lunch menu. A few seconds later, someone jumped up onto the barstool next to me and offered a vibrant, "Bonjour!" I glanced over at the sweaty man, wearing a worn leather cowboy hat who strongly resembled Jean-Claude Van Damme.

I was so transfixed by his face, I didn't realize at first, if I looked a bit further south, I would notice that this guy's only attire was that cowboy hat. With a small man purse on his lap hiding the front part of his nether regions, his naked butt was squished and sweating all over the barstool he sat on. He continued to smile at me in the most politely creepy way. Thankfully, I saw the love of my life walking from the bathroom just then. He quickly summed up my predicament with an amused smirk on his face. I jumped off the chair, bid the nude dude a fervent, "Au revoir," and we exited the bar area with our drinks in hand.

Back on the sand, we relaxed under an umbrella on two loungers while taking in the blissful sounds of people laughing, sweet calypso music in the distance, boats zooming back and forth on the open sea, and the waves crashing on the shore. As beachside ordering service was available, we decided to order lunch a little later and just relaxed with our drinks for the time being. It was such a euphoric moment that I must have dozed off for a bit while my then-fiancé went to get us more drinks at the bar. The next thing I knew, my barely opened eyes were staring directly at a penis! All I could think was, "Qu'est-ce que c'est?" (What the HECK is this?)

I sat up, frantic and startled. Adjusting my sunglasses and mentally willing that dangly thing out of my personal space, I stared up into the charismatic face of a trés French waiter. As if mirroring my barstool guy, he only wore one piece of clothing: a bowtie. I'm no prude, but I was still speechless. He held out a clipboard with the menu order forms ready to be completed. He asked in very stiff manner (no pun intended) if I would like to place an order. I stammered and quickly said in French, "Merci, mais pas maintenant." He bowed slightly, turned, and walked over to other beachgoers, buns of steel and all. Right then and there, I decided I really didn't want to eat from a restaurant where sweaty, salty butts (and other parts) had sat in the chairs and barstools before me.

For those who are dying to ask, "how was he hanging?", all I'll say is that you need to get to Orient Beach, St. Martin and get the answers to that question for yourself!

—R—
ROWDY AND
RIDICULOUS
MILLENNIALS

L ong before using the word "millennial" became a daily norm, I hosted a group of young dotcom millionaires from California. Under age 30 at the time, three of the five couples had experienced varying levels of extreme success within the tech world in a very short period of time. Some were household names. The main guest, Guy Goldberg, was the kingpin money man and his "friends" definitely knew how to take advantage of this.

The first night they arrived was... amusing. Two groupies in particular (the staff secretly joked that the duo looked like a George Michael/Andrew Ridgeley remake) were obnoxious on steroids. They weren't paying for squat, but consistently complained about everything simply for the fun of it. Bottles of wine weren't acceptably chilled, the just-picked bouquets weren't fresh enough, the Bose sound system wasn't loud enough, the 1500-square foot pool deck wasn't big enough... they went on and on. Mr. Goldberg just laughed at their gripes and told the staff to appease them. Too busy cozying up to a buxom redhead, he wasn't too bothered about what his friends were doing. But he soon would wish he had paid attention!

On the third day of the group's stay, I walked into my office building to find the chronic complainers from the first night were sitting at the concierge desk like employees. The blonde gentlemen shrieked with delight when they saw me and jumped out of the chairs to hug me. Taken aback by the affection of these virtual strangers, while still wondering how long they'd been in the office, and more importantly, HOW they'd gotten in there to begin with, I gently disengaged with a terse smile and asked how I could help them.

Dressed in crisp white short shorts and polo shirts, their perfectly glossed lips —a la Todd Chrisley—began to spit requests of grandeur. That day's big ask: a yacht to sail to St. Barths, but not just any yacht. It had to be the biggest yacht we could find in the area, with a crew. I told them that it was a bit late to find such a vessel for that very afternoon, but perhaps we could find one for the following day. When asked about the preferred budget, they looked at each other and guffawed into perfectly manicured hands. "Honey, money is no object! We have money, what we don't have is a big ass yacht, so make it happen."

When I asked whose credit card would be used to secure the reservation, they told me, "Mr. Goldberg's! And while you're working on that, please have seven more bottles of the Dom Perignon we had last night delivered to us on the pool deck. Also, we'd like the chef to stay at the villa all day today... we're going to parrrtayyyy." With that, they skipped out of the office and disappeared from sight.

I was more than skeptical about doing any of this on their say-so. The concierge wasn't scheduled to arrive for another hour, so I arranged both the yacht and the champagne myself. I decided to also call Guy Goldberg and apprise him of all the requests his buddies had made. He seemed a bit surprised, but didn't say no. After confirming that the 92-foot Sunseeker would be ready for 9 a.m. the following morning with final boarding call at 10 a.m., I also relayed that a cancellation fee of $4000 would be charged to his American Express on file if they decided to cancel for any reason. Lastly, I told him he would need to sign the documents I'd emailed to him confirming all the details of our phone conversation. He did so while I was still on the line, and after that call, I felt extremely accomplished for having only been at work for two hours.

The next day was all sunshine and calm shimmering sea. Our esteemed guests had certainly picked a gorgeous day for some fun on the water. The staff was on site early to help the party animals get to the yacht on time. Taxis were lined up and rearing to go. But, alas, the perfect day was not to be. The busty redhead who was Guy's main squeeze had been sick all night and did not want to step foot on a boat. Guy, in his chivalrous glory, refused to leave her side. The other guests were pleading with him to go on the trip to St. Barths anyway, but he paid them no mind. The friends who were trespassing in our offices the day before were especially irate with Guy. They refused to go unless he joined the group. (I bet they'd already calculated that without their walking ATM, they'd have to pay for lunch at Nikki Beach or perhaps pay for their own selections at Hermès and Luis Vuitton while shopping in Gustavia.).

In the end, as they stood there arguing and debating whether to send the redhead in a cab to our local clinic, time flew by. I received a call from one very unhappy boat captain. In his super thick Australian accent, he demanded to know why no one had boarded the yacht when it was already 10:15. I quickly put him on hold and asked the guests if they were going or not. They decided to cancel. While the captain swore in anger, he quickly reminded me that he would expect the cancellation fee to be paid within 48 hours before abruptly disconnecting the call.

Whatever Mr. Goldberg's girlfriend had going on was serious enough for the group to leave the island early. With plans to leave the very next morning, I prepared their final incidentals bill—around $12,000—and sent to Mr. Goldberg for his signature. Any incidental bill over $10,000 required a signature. He didn't send it back right away, so I figured I'd collect the signed copy before they checked out.

When I got to work on the morning of their departure, the disheveled group was already filing into the large luxury passenger van. I went into my office to see if the signed paperwork was on my desk. Nope, it wasn't. I called Mr. Goldberg's cell phone and asked him where the signed incidentals bill was. In an arrogantly nonchalant tone, he told me he didn't recognize most of the charges and therefore wasn't signing it. Then he hung up on me. Ummm...what???

I stared at the phone in disbelief and immediately made a few fast and furious phone calls. This may work on the US mainland, mister dotcom superstar, but not in the Caribbean...and not with me! Within 10 minutes, the van was back at the property. I walked out to meet it, with the document and a pen. Guy exited the bus and gave me a look that could melt a glacier as he scribbled his signature then proceeded to throw the pen and paper at me. As he marched back into the waiting van, I just threw my head back and laughed while the entire group peered at me through the tinted windows.

What did I do to make Guy Goldberg have such a sudden change of heart? How about making a call to the Chief Immigration Officer and the Chief Minister's office, asking them to stop those entitled cheapskates from leaving the island if they didn't sign? I then called back the taxi driver and asked him to put the call on speaker. I told the group that if their final bill was not signed by Mr. Goldberg, they would all be detained at the port and possibly arrested.

Moral of the story: If you don't want your AMEX card charged for $12,000 during your Caribbean vacation, monitor the greedy leeches you call friends. Sometimes they can do more harm than you could ever imagine. Just ask the family of Shanquella Robinson.

—S—

SANTERÍA SUITCASE

For those of us who remember what travel was like in a pre-9/11 world, nostalgic memories abound. No intrusive TSA screenings, bottled water and other liquids were allowed in carry-on luggage, loved ones could walk you right to your departure gate in many instances and you could pack just about anything in a suitcase with attractive weight limits. In some instances, people took the, "pack just about anything part," quite literally.

As I mentioned in an earlier chapters, I was blessed to work for a few different airlines during my hospitality career. While I enjoyed the hotel and private villa experiences, my airline jobs were the icing on the cake. Coming from a family of pilots, I loved airplanes from the moment I knew what they were. And due to my parents being from one Caribbean island while raising us on another island, we got to island hop every summer to see our very large family—a luxury many children didn't have in the 80's. That only stoked the fire in me to work in airlines one day. And so, I did.

While working at Miami International Airport for Cayman Airways in the late 90's, I had the pleasure of being a lead passenger agent for the Cuban flights. These flights were routed from Havana to Grand Cayman and then to Miami and vice-versa. There were no direct flights between the island and the United States back then. The flights operated only one day a week, and were always packed—whether inbound or outbound.

Working on those days offered more than just an opportunity for me to practice my Spanish. I learned a lot about Cuban culture and demographics, too. For example, up until then, 90% of the Cubans I knew in Florida were white. I had no idea that so many black Cubans existed until I worked the flights.

Back to this story...

One of the things we had to do as part of the flight clearance for inbound flights from Cuba was go down into the Customs and Immigration area. We had to be present in the baggage claim area just in case anything wonky happened and passengers would have to be sent back without leaving the airport for whatever reason. It rarely happened, but protocols were protocols.

As part of my training, I would go down into the bowels of the airport with a manager or supervisor to learn the ropes. On the day in question, the Cuban flight was particularly problematic. Several suitcases were flagged and we were called to witness the Customs inspections. My trainer moved effortlessly through the throngs of people while I struggled to keep up. We finally arrived at the screening area and an innocent-looking grandma stood there with a firm grip on her hand luggage and a fierce resilience in her eyes. Dressed in mostly white, her smooth mocha face and wavy waist-length salt and pepper hair belied her age of 72, per her passport.

The Customs inspector instructed us to put on gloves and open her suitcase to assist with the search. Strange as that seemed, being just a trainee, I followed orders. My colleague, however, told me to stand back as she proceeded to handle the task alone. Boy, was I ever glad she did.

As she tumbled the clothes and shoes in the overstuffed green suitcase, the abuela started mumbling in Spanish, but I couldn't understand what she was saying. Sounded like prayers, but it wasn't clear enough for me to be sure. About two minutes later, my coworker jumped back as if stuck by something sharp. She pointed to something in a jar and asked the Customs guy to take it out. Curiously, I stepped closer and peeked at what had spooked her. The clear bottle, like a large glass jar of mayo that was rinsed clean, held a dark, reddish-brown liquid with various thin white sticks and what looked like pebbles.

My brain could not compute what I was looking at, and grandma was acting like someone had just slapped her in the face. The Customs officer and the passenger had a heated exchange in Spanish and the only words I understood were religion, santería, blood and chicken bones. I wanted to pass out. Was I understanding this correctly or were my Spanish translation brain cells broken?

This woman had just imported some black magic hocus pocus crap in her suitcase! Now I'd seen it all. Was she going to put a spell on us for having disturbed her accoutrements? Lord have mercy...I sure hoped not. I started mumbling some Jesus prayers of my own! This was insane. I'd learned about santería in my Religions of The World class that very semester at college, so I was equal parts intrigued and terrified. Santería, a fusion of elements of Catholicism and Yoruba / West African religions, is widely practiced in Cuba and other parts of the world. Akin to what some would call voodoo or obeah in the Caribbean, santería is seen as equally dark and taboo by many.

Nevertheless, after probably scaring the daylights out of the Customs officer, the elegant woman smiled as he zipped up her suitcase and waved her on her way. I wondered who was going to get the heebie-jeebies put on them by that deceptively cute and innocent grandma. I was thankful it would not be me!

—T—

TIP TRIP

This chapter is about how people react to tipping, both guests and staff, how I've seen it become either a blessing or a curse during my career.

Tips are vital in the hospitality industry. Many workers earn low hourly wages and tips help to bridge the gap financially. In some establishments, like in most Caribbean hotels and restaurants, a mandatory service charge is automatically added to guest bills and distributed among the staff at a designated time, whether at the end of each day or on a specific date during the month. However, a tip is separate and apart from the service charge and goes a long way in showing appreciation to staff. While not mandatory, tipping is usually expected and is often the subject of contentious drama.

First case in point... A renowned music executive who rubbed shoulders with the likes of Jay Z, Mariah Carey, and other world-famous artists on the regular was getting ready to check out of a private villa one morning. He called me to his suite, and when I arrived, he and his girlfriend were sitting on the bed, counting hundred-dollar bills and stuffing envelopes with various employee names written on each one. I'd given him a list of names of his personal staff the day before, and while I thought it was such a nice gesture, I was curious to know what he wanted now.

When he opened his mouth, I tried my best to smile and squash the urge to give a dreaded eye-roll. He proceeded to say, "I've got some tips in these envelopes for the staff. Now I want to make sure that I take care of my people. I want to give them tips like they've never seen before. They gonna be jumping up and down when they tear open these envelopes! So, I need you to tell me if it's too much...I wanna be the biggest tipper they've ever seen. They won't forget me after today!"

I frowned at that moment because it was not my place to tell this man how much to tip. While it was his personal choice and a nice gesture, it was not a competition. When I told him and his girlfriend that the staff would be ecstatic, they both gave me a dazzlingly perfect smile. I know they felt good about what they had done, and the staff would get some extra cash as well. I stayed silent as he went on the tell me he'd put $300 in each of the eight envelopes. While I knew $300 was a considerable gift, I couldn't dare tell that wealthy music exec that some staff members had received tips of over $2000 each.

Second case in point... I recall scenarios where a specific team, of maybe five or six employees, worked together for a group event or with a very large family. When it was time for the guests to leave, only certain staff members received tips while others did not. I don't know if the ones who got the tips were just daft or inherently wicked, but they would often tear open their envelopes in front of everyone, then ask the others, "How much did you get?" Sometimes the somber answer was, "Nothing. We got nothing." And then petty drama ensued. I cannot begin to tell you how many arguments and brawls stemmed from such incidents. I felt like I was stuck in the middle of a dreadful soap opera when those situations arose.

The flip side of the tipping game are the times when staff expected tips and there were none whatsoever. Some guests, no matter how great the service was, and regardless of the staff going above and beyond for them, never left a dime in tip money. Those were the times when staff assumed tips had been left and either taken by their fellow staff members or by management.

An element of distrust prevailed when it came to tips. While I knew for a fact that some senior managers and general managers at other properties heartlessly stole tips from the hourly staff without a hint of remorse, I was not wired that way. Besides my family having multiple longstanding businesses and me earning money passively through those companies during my hospitality career, I had no urge or desire to steal from anyone. On the contrary, there were times when departing guests had marched up to my office with Thank You cards or envelopes full of money...just for me! And what would I do? I'd go to the bank on my lunch break, get smaller bills and divvy it up among the staff. I didn't have to, but I enjoyed doing it.

Some upper management colleagues called me foolish to my face. But I didn't care. I always felt it was the right thing to do. "Teamwork makes the dream work," as they say. The irony in those situations was that I'd later hear grumblings and rumors of how I'd "stolen" the tip money and had only given "a pittance" to the staff. It didn't even make sense to explain and clear my name. I realized early on that once you become a senior manager, you become fair game to whatever nasty little lies wicked and jealous people cook up.

I end this chapter with a tip of my own: I've said before, this industry is not one in which you can survive being thin-skinned. I've been maligned, discredited, lied on, given a cutesy souvenir doll that was supposed to hurt me (a "nice gift" from a voodoo-loving employee from Dominica who hated her strict boss...aka me), and countless other assaults on my sanity and health. But here I am...in all my sane, blessed and happy glory, sharing my experiences with the world. Resilience, a sound mind, and a strong resolve are cumulatively needed to succeed in the upper echelons of hospitality management. That's non-negotiable!

—U—

UNDERCOVER
INSPECTORS

There is so much that goes on behind the scenes in the hotel industry. All the working parts, both visible and invisible, go hand in hand to ensure that guests are pampered and satisfied during their stay. One aspect of this is the dreaded undercover inspector.

I personally don't mind inspections and think they are necessary. However, a property could be having a week from hell for whatever reason (broken equipment, sick staff, recovering from a weather event, late or delayed shipments) and, voila, an inspector shows up.

My initial firsthand experience with an inspector was at Sheriva Villas. A gentleman called the office one morning and said he was on the island, had had a mix-up at another hotel, and wanted a room for only one night. It was actually the last day before we closed for the late summer/fall break which typically ran from August to October; the property was literally empty. I told him that a suite for the night would be $800. He simply asked, "Do you take AMEX?"

After finishing that very brief call with my soon-to-be guest, I told the only housekeeper on duty to prep a Grand master suite for the new arrival later that afternoon. The butler quickly whipped up some hors d'oeuvres and a pitcher of rum punch. After making sure all the tech items were functioning and the pool was clean, we waited for the guest to show up.

At about 3 p.m. a taxi pulled up and a Raymond Reddington doppelganger stepped out (If you're not a Blacklist fan, you'll have to Google dear old Red to understand). He even wore a fedora hat with his tropical print shirt, khaki shorts, and flip flops. He said a cordial hello to the staff and wandered into the villa, leaving his suitcase at the base of the stairs. The butler quickly took it inside and gave him a welcome orientation as I ran his credit card back in the office.

By the time I walked back over, the gentleman was already in the pool, smoking a cigar with music blasting. I asked him if he needed chef service for that evening. He assured me he was fine and that he had made his own dinner arrangements. When I asked him about breakfast service, he told me he'd given the butler his request for bran cereal and 2% milk to be left in the refrigerator with a pot of coffee ready by 8 a.m. His plan was to check out by 10 a.m. I bid him a good evening and left the premises.

The next morning, he strolled into our main lobby looking quite different from the man who'd stepped out of the cab the day before. The man who stood before me was dressed in a crisp long-sleeved shirt and tie with long dress pants and loafers. It was a strange transformation considering I assumed he was on vacation and needed a quick one-night before checking into another property for a longer stay. That sort of thing happened from time to time.

Something told me this was different. He smiled and handed me a business card. When I read it, my eyes opened wide. He was a AAA Inspector! I smiled and asked him how we did. He beamed as he told me he was pleased to confirm that we'd just earned AAA Four Diamond status. I jumped for joy as he showed me the report with all the metrics and observations. It was A LOT! From running his hands over the top of the refrigerator to test for dust to measuring the speed of the internet and the quality of the water in the pool, he had probably spent much of the previous evening doing his job without us ever knowing. He even noted on the report how he'd left his suitcase behind when he stepped out of the cab, just to test how efficient the staff would be.

It was cool to have passed the inspection with flying colors, especially at the tail end of the season. And we earned that distinction for many years thereafter with other inspectors. Inspectors don't announce they're coming, they simply show up. It reminded me and our entire team to always be ready for that walk-in guest. You never know who he—or she—might really be.

—V—

VISCOUNT DI MONTO-VERONA

My mom taught me many things, but one vital phrase I carry with me daily is: "Deal with people according to knowledge." Doing this has served me well over the years.

One experience where this came in especially handy was dealing with one Mr. di Monto-Verona. I knew he would be trouble the moment I took his initial call. The man exuded a nauseating arrogance from our very first interaction. He immediately alluded to his British-Italian royal lineage in the first five minutes of that fateful phone call. He stressed the need for perfection for his family of three who would be flying in from London. His wife and six-year-old son would be joining him for the week.

After wrapping up that discovery call, I emailed his confirmation letter with the property's terms and deposit instructions. He returned the signed documents three days later and everything was set. He was due to arrive in two months, so I'd literally forgotten about him until the week of his arrival, which was the Thursday before Easter.

On the Tuesday of that week, I received a phone call from the self-proclaimed aristocrat. In a nasally exaggerated British accent, he asked, "At what time shall we be allowed to check in tomorrow? I'd like to arrive a bit earlier so that we can frolic on the beach before sunset."

Perplexed, I quickly pulled up his reservation and noted his arrival date. I gently reminded him that his arrival day was Thursday, not Wednesday. He detonated into a massive tirade about lawsuits and bad publicity if I didn't have his villa ready for him when he arrived the following day. I simply listened and let him rant. We were fully booked at the property until Thursday morning, so it was not even an option to add an extra night to his reservation. But even if I did, why would I want to help a moron who was launching lawsuit threats when he was clearly in the wrong?

When he was finished, I told him, "Sir, you booked this reservation months ago. You and I both have signed copies of credit card receipt with the dates noted on that form. Your arrival date is not tomorrow, and I do not have a villa available for an early check in. If you'd like suggestions on nearby properties for one night, I'd be happy to provide options."

He grumbled and threatened a bit longer and, in a huff, hung up. At that stage in my career, I had become somewhat numb to the idiotic behavior of entitled adults. I sighed and immediately sent an eblast to the staff and property owners. Pulling from my experience, I knew this guest was going to be problematic. I shared my thoughts in the email, including what had just taken place, and told everyone to be on the lookout for this deranged man in case he showed up the next day. Luckily, he did not. Unfortunately for us, he still showed up on the correct day with his family.

They were an odd trio. The wife's cold demeanor, tight Nordic facial features, and statuesque frame immediately earned her the moniker, "Ice Queen", by the staff. The notorious Viscount, barely a few inches over five feet tall, and almost as many feet wide, seemed to have a permanent grimace, even as he was being served delectable canapés and a refreshing rum punch overlooking the Caribbean Sea. His midnight hair and small narrow eyes matched his brooding personality perfectly.

A ray of sunshine, the lanky son's 1000-watt smile overrode his parents' miserable attitudes. Such a bubbly child, he loved the crab races the butler organized for him and all the pool toys we provided for him. At least, he seemed genuinely overjoyed to be in the land of sun and sea.

Over the next few days, the family did what most families do on vacation: swim, eat, explore, relax, repeat. Until one evening when all hell broke loose. Around sunset on Easter Monday, a raving Mr. di Monto-Verona ran into our main lobby holding his son in his arms, blood dripping on the pristine marble tiles. Several of us ran to his side asking what had happened, how serious were the injuries, and if we should call an ambulance. He ignored our questions, and in an expressionless manner, said, "I will be filing a lawsuit. I need you to tell me exactly **WHO** I should be suing."

Bewildered by his statement, I vehemently implored, "Your son is crying, and bleeding, and your only concern is a lawsuit? **WHAT HAPPENED?**"

As his wife approached carrying beach bags, looking harried, he rapidly told us that his son had been walking along the beach when a broken piece of glass had sliced through his foot. He told us to call an ambulance. In the meantime, one of the staff members had used items from a first aid kit to staunch the child's bleeding while another person began cleaning the floors. Our administrative manager, after calling the ambulance, walked up to Mrs. di Monto-Verona and offered what she thought were comforting words, "It's not as bad as it seems. See, he's even stopped crying. The ambulance will be here shortly, and everything will be alright, sweetheart."

No one was prepared for what happened next.

The Viscountess inhaled sharply, clenched fists jammed to her side, and screamed in her posh uppity Brit accent, "Don't you **DARE** call me **SWEETHEART!** How **DARE** you refer to me as "**SWEETHEART**"??? I am Viscountess di Monto-Verona to **YOU**, and I demand to speak to your manager **NOW!**" Welp! I immediately rushed over and stood in front of my colleague for fear the towering woman would hit her.

Our distraught admin manager had no idea that her well-meaning words would be taken as an insult. She retreated to her office in shocked silence after offering a sincere apology. Knowing it was truly not professional to call a guest, "sweetheart," I also knew that culturally, in the Caribbean, words like "darling" and "sweetheart," even when used to address strangers, were meant to show kindness and hospitality. I tried to explain this to the enraged woman while continuing to apologize, but she wouldn't listen. She instead rudely asked me why I was speaking to her when she'd asked for the manager.

Repeating her demands to speak to the manager, it was my turn to get a bit prickly, as I said, "You asked for the manager, and here I am. Unfortunate as it is, your son was hurt on a public beach. You and your husband decided to drive back to our office with a bleeding child and the first words uttered were about filing a lawsuit, not 'we need help.' My colleagues and I are assisting you in every way possible, and while I absolutely apologize for how you were just addressed, I can assure you that one, it was not meant in disrespect, and two, it will not happen again."

She scowled at me like I was dog poop under her shoes and swiftly turned her back to me. Glancing in her, now silent, husband's direction, she told him to pick up the boy again so they could head back to their villa. When we asked them what to do about the ambulance that was already en-route, they simply ignored us all and trotted off. When the ambulance arrived, we directed it to the villa, but in less than two minutes it drove away. Apparently, they had refused medical help. I truly felt sorry for the little boy.

The next day, as predicted, the Viscount sent an email stating that he wished to pursue legal action against SOMEONE for this son being hurt. I smiled as I read the letter because I knew once I forwarded it to our CEO, Mr. di Monto-Verona would regret ever stepping foot on the property and issuing such an asinine threat. The property owner wore many hats and was socially well-connected, particularly in the legal world. Having a five-star property was a fantastic achievement, but that status also attracted opportunists of every kind. Our CEO had prepared meticulously for any eventuality that could result in legal action from a guest, including ones with what I assumed to be a fake title (we later found out that, for a hefty price, people could buy a peerage title on sites like The Manorial Society of Great Britain). Not only would the miserable man not get a dime, but he had also earned the distinction of being added to our infamous **DNA (DO NOT ACCEPT)** List. Now, that's what I'd call a royal honor!

W
WEEKEND ON A WHIM

Years ago, when I was helping to run our family business on St. Croix, burnout became so real, I could not focus or function. I knew I needed a break and the only antidote for me was to retreat to the comfort and sanctity of my family's cabin on Anguilla for a week. One weekend, on a whim, I decided to grab two tickets on the Caribbean airline, LIAT, to fly to St. Maarten and then hop on a 20-minute ferry to Anguilla. The flight would be a quick 35-minute jaunt from St. Croix to St. Maarten on a sunny afternoon. I envisioned having a divine grilled snapper lunch at Enoch's in Marigot, St. Martin and then dinner on Anguilla in my pj's would round out the day. Simple enough plan, right? **WRONG!**

On the day of our trip, my husband and I each packed a backpack, and checked one suitcase. We arrived at the ticket counter, greeted the airline staff. and were promptly given an unusual update: the flight would now be making a stop in the British Virgin Islands before heading to St. Maarten. A broad grin appeared on my face as I turned to the hubster and said, "Wouldn't it be great if we could overnight there and see our friends in Tortola?" I was already dreaming of bubbling hot rock oven pizza from The Watering Hole and the best cup of coffee from Omar's Café (formerly D'Best Cup)! I'd done this before, and it would be easy to continue with the next leg of our trip the following day with no problems. But when I asked about it, the desk agent said it could not be done... at least not for free. And I wasn't in the mood to fork over another $150.

As we prepared to leave St. Croix, the TSA process wrapped up quickly and we eventually boarded the two-hours delayed LIAT flight. The airline's steadfast unofficial motto of, Leave Island Any Time, rang faithfully true that day. I put that behind me and felt the thrill of having the opportunity to fly over the heavenly BVI once again.

We took off, and in 20 minutes, the islands —that make so many others pale in comparison—came into view. We landed on Beef Island, Tortola and I again started dreaming of how much FUN it would be just to stay there for 24 hours. The plane powered down and we waited for more passengers to board.

In the meantime, a rusty blue pickup truck parked alongside the ATR aircraft and, all of a sudden, a guy started piling luggage into the back of it. I watched this, feeling quite anxious and thought to myself, "That couldn't be our bright burgundy suitcase peeking from the bottom of that mountainous pile, could it?" Nah...couldn't be. I even asked my husband if he thought that little tip of maroon was our suitcase and he said, "No!"

I tried to relax in the now unpleasantly warm aircraft, while stifling a laugh as the elderly but feisty Trinidadian woman seated in front of us started bawling about her severe hunger. Animatedly, she spoke loudly and firmly, "Listen here, I hungry. Hungry bad. Meh belly growlin'. Allyuh betta hurry up and get dis plane off the ground and let me get to Trinidad safe, fast, and in a hurry."

She then pointed out of the tiny window and blatantly let everyone on board know that if her suitcase, clearly visible on the truck, didn't make it to Trinidad that night, it would be "hell to tell the priest." She provided all the onboard entertainment we needed as we smoldered for another five minutes.

At this point, we saw a long line of passengers emerge from the tiny Beef Island terminal. I didn't pay much attention to the quantity of people until I realized the line literally wrapped around one side of the aircraft. I glanced around at the empty seats behind us and in front of us and grimaced. There was NO WAY all those people were going to fit on this flight.

I whispered those thoughts to my love and said, "If they want volunteers to stay here, we are jumping up immediately!" The passengers started to file in. Eventually the flight attendant nearest to us started to frown. Then she began to walk back and forth frantically, as if hoping extra seats would magically appear. I began to grin from ear to ear.

A second flight attendant came over the PA system and requested volunteers. They confirmed that they would be paying for round trip transportation between the airport and a hotel, plus dinner and breakfast. My husband sprang into action, and made it to the rear of the aircraft and ever-so-kindly volunteered first. I could hardly contain myself. The only thing I wasn't doing was cartwheels in the aisle. Woohoooo! Yessssss... I got our hand luggage out, waved goodbye to the other passengers, especially my new Trini grandma, and headed to the rear of the aircraft. When I got to the exit door, my husband turned and looked at me with dismay. What now?? I quickly found out. The flight attendant had asked him if we had checked luggage, he'd said yes, and she then said, "Sorry, we have to take these two passengers who have no bags. Sorry, Mr. and Mrs. Gittens." NOOOOOO! The heartbreak. The anger. The disappointment. No sushi at Origin? Really????!!!!

I made my walk of shame back to our seats and sat glumly as the pilots finally got some airco pumping once again. In a short five minutes, we were taxiing down the runway, and back on our way to St. Maarten. A somber 25 minutes later, we landed in St. Maarten. We got through Immigration with ease and stared at the belt awaiting our single suitcase. There were nine other people there as well who'd been on our flight. By that time, they'd missed their connections to the USA and Europe and were frantic to get information on when they would be able to leave St. Maarten.

It was then 6:15 p.m. I went to the restroom and walked back out to see everyone still staring at the belt. Still no luggage. I was beginning to have a sinking feeling in the pit of my stomach. What if that really was our suitcase left behind in Tortola? Did I just lose a free mini vacation for nothing???

It soon became totally clear that this was exactly the case. I WAS LIVID! We had no luggage and the last ferry to Anguilla from St. Martin was at 7 p.m. I glanced at my watch. I saw that it was already 6:40 and knew we couldn't make it to Marigot on the French side of the island in time. I simply had no fight left in me. We decided we'd have to grab a hotel room as I didn't feel like bothering any of my family on St. Maarten for a quick overnight. Besides, we'd have to come back to the airport the next day to hunt down our suitcase. My backpack had a scanty smorgasbord of items including a t-shirt and make-up, but no undies or toiletries (so much for being savvy travelers!).

We stood around for another 15 minutes waiting for an airline rep to assist us. No one came. The other airlines were closing their luggage assistance desks for the evening and could care less about LIAT's angry passengers. I finally saw one of my cousins who just happened to be working late and asked him if he could please hunt down someone from this very exceptional airline to assist us with lost luggage reports.

At approximately 6:58 p.m., a lanky young man nonchalantly sauntered up to our small crowd and asked, "Who's first? I need all your bag claim tags, so please have them out." I immediately started to search through my handbag for my claim tag while the other passengers were being assisted. I figured they had bigger issues, as I was pretty much already at home just by being on St. Maarten.

No matter how deep I dug, I couldn't find my bag claim tags. Just then, I suddenly and VIVIDLY remembered that our gate agent on St. Croix had torn off the side of our boarding pass that he'd stuck our bag claim tag to. I groaned inwardly and wanted to scream. I was 0 for 3... no free night on Tortola, no way to get to Anguilla that night and now a missing suitcase with no claim ticket to file the lost luggage report.

When I finally got to the counter, the young man chuckled when I explained to him that I had no bag claim ticket. He told me it would be ok. Earlier I had heard him telling the other passengers that they would be put into a hotel for the night and rebooked on flights to New York, Miami, and Paris the next day, hoping that their luggage would appear early enough to go with them.

I asked him if we would be offered a hotel stay for the night as well, even though we had no onward connection by plane. He called the airline supervisor on the phone. After a series of smirks and eye rolls, I knew the answer was no. He hung up the phone and said that his supervisor said it was not possible. I frowned and started to open my mouth to go ballistic on the young man, but instead said, "I don't see how that's fair. We were all equally inconvenienced by your airline. I guess it's true that Caribbean people really don't give a crap about other Caribbean people. Can you just ask the supervisor to at least call and book us a room at the hotel where everyone else is staying? Hopefully, he can get us a lower rate."

We exited the baggage claim area and went in search of this asinine supervisor. We found him having a beer at a kiosk (astute professional!). I again asked if the airline would also accommodate us for the night. Not only were we inconvenienced due to their late arrival and overbooking of the flight, but now we would be further financially inconvenienced. He said he was sorry, but they could only accommodate passengers who had onward flights out of St. Maarten. He agreed to book the hotel for us but warned that the rate was a bit high for just a quick overnight. He offered us a more affordable option at another hotel that was fairly gross and in a seedy part of town. I gave him a solid HELL NO and told him to book the hotel where everyone else was staying and we'd deal with it. He stared at me blankly and said he would book the room and get us the free shuttle to the property. I thanked him for his "ample generosity."

As we walked away, I could feel him staring at us. I couldn't tell if it was pity or shock that we were not biting his Heineken-filled head off. He then shouted at us to wait a moment and pointed to a row of seats where we could sit and wait as we joined the other stuck passengers...a lively mix of French, American, Chilean, and Dutch tourists who'd been in the British Virgin Islands on vacation. We were soon told the hotel van would pick us up in a few minutes. I closed my eyes and said a quick prayer. Thankful to be safe and sound, regardless of the myriad inconveniences.

At that point, while awaiting the shuttle, my husband went to get us some drinks. I started to text my family on St. Croix to let them know what was happening when the airline supervisor walked up to me and said, "Ma'am, we are going to take care of your hotel room this evening. Dinner and breakfast will be included also." It was my turn to just stare at him. I had no idea what had transpired to make this happen, but I couldn't hide my joy. When the hubby returned seconds later, and I told him about our new and improved situation. He just hit me with that million-dollar smile as I grabbed my cocktail and took a sip, grinning.

On our way to the hotel, we were told that the recently refurbished beachfront property had 24/7 front desk service and washers and dryers in most rooms. I couldn't believe my ears. We could actually wash our grimy clothes! A small but well-stocked supermarket was around the corner that opened until 11:30 p.m. so we could purchase toiletries and other knickknacks. The night was definitely looking up!

As we pulled into the hotel entrance, there was a tiny ranch-looking restaurant next door area with flashing neon lights. Tacky was an understatement. We were told by the driver that we would have a nice dinner there, courtesy of the airline. I was already thinking, "There must be a better restaurant around here somewhere?" That place looked like something you'd find in the middle of a dusty border town in Texas, not in one of the gourmet dining capitals of the Caribbean.

Nevertheless, we checked in and went straight to our room. Nice, clean, A/C already pumping, safe in the closet, kitchenette, spacious balcony, iron and ironing board. But wait, no washer and dryer? We hit every little nook and cranny in search of the elusive duo. My husband fiddled with a single door in the center of our suite, thinking perhaps the washer and dryer were behind it. However, when the door swung open, we were staring into another guest suite.

Quickly taking it in, we noted the rumpled beds and empty wine bottles on the tables. Timidly crossing over into the seemingly vacant room, we could smell the sea through the ajar balcony door. Used towels were scattered throughout. It was a much larger suite than ours with a full kitchen and dining room. After being nosy for a few more seconds, lo and behold, tucked into a little alcove, was that wonderful duo we were searching for: the washer and dryer! We retreated into our own room and pondered our potential good fortune. But what if other guests were staying there?

My hotel General Manager-radar kicked in at that moment. I went back into the other suite to investigate, room by room. No luggage, no food in the fridge, no personal items or toiletries in the oversized bathroom, no real sign of anyone staying there. I concluded it was probably a check-out room that the housekeepers hadn't gotten to yet. And what a groovy convenience that was for us. Can I get an "amen"? Even though the room was not clean, the washer and dryer seemed to work just fine. And that's all we needed.

We decided to go grab our complimentary dinner at tacky-central and then make a stop at the corner store right after. If we returned to the second suite and it remained as is, we'd wash our clothes and go to sleep as happy campers. Right before we left our floor, however, my husband pulled a quick 007 move and put the DO NOT DISTURB sign on the other suite's door. We prayed that no one would come into that room—at least not until we did some laundry.

Dinner at the rustic little restaurant was absolutely superb. I had a big piece of humble pie that night. Never judge a book by its cover. The menu, a fusion of Mexican/Venezuelan cuisine, also offered dishes with hints of Colombian flair. Best steak fajitas I've ever had. PERIOD! My husband, who is actually from South America, relished every bite of his melt-in-your-mouth ribeye. If you're a red meat lover, you know South Americans do it best.

After dinner, filled and happy, we walked to the mini-mart and purchased necessary toiletries and snacks.

When we returned to our suite, nothing had changed. When God opens doors of favor (literally!), we need to walk through those doors with confidence.

We showered, washed our clothes and went to sleep being so grateful. In that moment, I truly understood what the bible verse about being thankful in all situations really meant. What had seemed like such an adverse situation actually led to a well-needed and entertaining distraction. The next morning, after a leisurely breakfast, we went back to the airport and there was our missing suitcase—freshly arrived from Tortola.

In that moment, I felt like we had experienced a divine prank. I'm a firm believer that God orders our steps—and our stops. We weren't meant to stay overnight on Tortola or go to Anguilla the night before. Instead, we had a fun misadventure on St. Maarten. It was a night we won't soon forget!

—X—
XXX

By now, especially if you read Book 1, and most of this book, you probably realize that much of the hotel and private villa sector is in some way affected by—and exposed to sex—in many ways. Sex tourism is big business—especially in the Caribbean. People travel exclusively for "sexcapades." They stay in bespoke hotels or extremely private villas to be free to do as they please. Strangely enough, once you've been in the industry a while, you see the signs of the kinky travelers a mile away. There are times, however, when things are so unexpectedly mindboggling, you can't forget them no matter how darn hard you try.

There was once a group of five—two men and three women—who arrived from Texas by private jet. They were the walking stereotype of Texans. The men shared loud, hearty laughs and wore big cowboy hats and jeans with boots. One man was probably in his late 30's while the other looked to be in his late 50's or early 60's. Two of the women, very petite and who looked to be of similarly matched ages to the two men, proudly displayed big hair and big personalities. The only one who looked out of place was a coquettish young woman in her 20's who stepped out of the taxi wearing a huge fur coat, gigantic gold hoop earrings, and blinged-out boots. In the Caribbean, in early fall, the temperatures are still in the high 80's or low 90's. I'd never seen anyone wear a fur coat in the islands. It was not only impractical, but it also looked ridiculous.

The group sauntered into their villa and immediately told us they had to watch football. Apparently, the younger of the two men was co-owner of one of the teams and wanted to see the game. Not all channels from the mainland USA were available in the islands at the time, but our I.T. Director knew what to do to make the guests happy. He was determined to get that channel up and running for our VIP guest.

Right before dinner, as I was about to leave for the day, the I.T. Director stepped into my office with a troubled, but amused, look on his face. He sat down in front of me without uttering a word. Busy doing something on my computer, I barely glanced up as I asked him what was going on. He just stared at me and started rubbing his head. This was feeling like déjà vu (see Book One, Chapter G) so I sat back, gave him my undivided attention, and got ready for the crap that I was about to hear. Sure enough, he got his bearings and told me a story that made me laugh out loud until tears of disbelief streamed down my face.

The story went a little something like this. The man and woman in their 30's was a married couple. The older couple was the parents of the 20-something girl. They'd brought the parents along at the request of the daughter in the fur coat. And here's where the young woman fit in:

The I.T. Director told me that shortly before sunset, he had finally gotten the channels up and running. When he called out to the main guest to tell him what he'd accomplished, he couldn't find him. He said he waited a while near the living room area, hoping the guest would appear so he could have a discussion with him and provide instructions on what to do with the tv channels. Instead, he said he heard laughter and voices behind the master bedroom door.

He took it upon himself to once again call out to the guest by name and ask him for a moment of his time. The man answered from behind the door and told the I.T. Director it was okay to open the door and come in. So, that's what he did. But what he saw when he opened the door is the stuff XXX movies are made of.

The fur coat-wearing diva was completely naked, and in bed with the other couple. They continued their sex play with him standing there. Not the slightest bit embarrassed that they were being seen by a member of staff, they instead turned to him, pausing only for a second, and asked him if he wanted to join in. Speechless, he said he backed out of the doorway and stammered a quick, "No thanks, I'm married. But you have a good time!" He then quickly closed the door and hightailed it outta there. He said the only thing he heard as he retreated was the deep and hearty laugh of Mr. Cowboy and the giggles of the two women. I could not believe my ears. I started to wonder if the parents of the young woman knew of the threesome's shenanigans.

The next morning, I saw the group, and had I not been told by my very trustworthy and honest colleague what he'd experienced the night before, there is no way I could have ever imagined such a thing. It truly made me realize how little we know about people. It also made me think of one of my cousin's favorite phrases: "Not my monkey, not my circus." What the guests did in the privacy of their rooms was their business. Not mine, not anyone else's. (Well, I guess that's true, except when you're being invited to join in, which I implore anyone NOT TO DO!)

—Y—
YEARNING FOR
BALANCE

One of the most frustrating and unavoidable things for anyone working in hospitality, is the fact that the industry never sleeps. This is something that eventually got to me over the years. When I was single, I'd work 60 to 70 hours a week at my airline jobs without thinking twice. I lived for the thrill, the travel benefits, and the overtime. It was FUN!

After I got married and had my sons, every holiday became an opportunity to make memories. But it usually meant I was absent from those memory-making moments. In typical hospitality fashion, I was always busiest during major holidays. Easter, Christmas, New Year's Eve, Thanksgiving... all the times of year where family bonding means so much... I was stuck at work.

Even with my husband's support and dedication, I felt horrible whenever I missed my kids' birthday parties, PTA meetings, and other milestones. I recall one December evening, on my way back to work from a Christmas concert at their elementary school, my husband and I got slammed by another car. While the accident wasn't our fault, it still felt like if I hadn't been rushing back to work, and instead had taken my boys out for ice cream after their cute little performances (like a "normal mom"), that accident would not have happened.

There was another incident that happened when my sons were about seven and five years old. I had to leave them alone for about ten minutes to get back to work. They were "driving" their new toy jeep and whizzing around our huge porch all afternoon. At around 5:15 p.m., I called my husband who said he was only five minutes away, that the boys would be fine, and I should head back to my office. I got dressed and sternly told my sons not to drive their toy jeep down the very steep concrete steps at the front of our house. I'd seen them attempt to do so once before and had threatened them then as well.

They uttered a very cute, "Yes, mommy," in unison, as I kissed them both before jumping into my car. This is the part where I might get slammed for leaving my kids alone at such a young age, but my dad was also at the house. It's just that asking him to look after the boys would have been pointless as we weren't on speaking terms (long story that could probably be another book on its own!).

I got back to my office just as the sun began to set. I'd literally just sat in my chair to boot up my computer, when my cell phone rang. My husband simply said, "Meet me at the hospital. I'm with the boys. They got hurt in the toy jeep." I dashed everything back into my briefcase and ran to my car. On the way to the hospital, speeding like a madwoman, I called my boss and told him I had to

74

go to the hospital and someone would have to cover for me tonight. There was no way I was going to leave my children again that night. I didn't even know how bad it was, and as much as I'd tried to call back my husband, his cell just rang and rang. Through tears of anguish, I made it the hospital in record time.

When I got to the ER, everyone at the tiny hospital was expecting me, so I quickly went through the double doors to find my sons. The older boy was inside with doctors and my husband while the younger one was sitting on a chair off to the side, alone. I hugged and kissed him and asked him to tell me what happened. He looked up at me sheepishly and his tiny voice, said, "We were disobedient, mommy. We went down the steps. My brother has a lot of blood on his head."

I could have died right then and there. I told my baby to sit quietly and not to move, while I tried to see my older son. My husband came out at that moment and told me that the doctors were finishing up the stitches on my older son's head. I could hear him screaming behind the curtains and I just kept calling out through my own flood of tears, "Mommy's here, honey. Mommy is right here." Apparently, he'd gashed his head when the toy jeep flipped on the very steps I'd told them to stay clear of. Boys will be boys, but that day was crazy on so many levels. I knew some drastic changes had to be made. I wanted a career, but I wanted my family more. If I had to put my dreams on hold to be there for my family, I would do just that.

I decided that very night that investing so much of my time ensuring other families were happy while together on a great vacation, was not quite worth me losing precious time with my own family. I made some requests at my job, and eventually got promoted. I found myself in a blessed position where I was no longer just on a weekly schedule but was the one making the weekly schedule. I took that opportunity and seniority to ensure I spent most holidays with my family, much to their delight. We enjoyed long weekends together and island-hopped. The children played on the beach for hours or swam in the pools at our hotels while my husband and I enjoyed each other's uninterrupted company. I visited with friends and family more often and it felt SO good. In those moments, I truly understood what work/life balance really meant.

Today, my sons are adults, and I spend a lot of time with them. We talk. We discuss and dissect things in our home. I asked them once how they felt about me working so hard when they were little and spending so many holidays at the office. They were honest in saying that sometimes they were upset that I was always working, but they did enjoy being with me after school in my office and hanging out in the fancy villas, and getting to play on the beach. They also said that visiting their grandma during the Christmas holidays was always fun because it was also Carnival there during that time of year. They loved to watch the boat parade and the bright, shiny costumes during the parade of troupes.

While I do feel guilty about the important dates I missed with my family, the fact that my boys—and my marriage —came through unscathed, makes me feel a whole lot better about having worked so hard. This industry isn't for everyone. The sacrifices are real, and burnout is inevitable. Be prepared for that.

—Z—
ZEN

The feeling of peace and calm is something every human craves (at least I hope so). Ultimately, one must be in tune with that inner voice and intuition to know how to maneuver this journey called life.

In the pursuit of peace and enlightenment, sometimes hard decisions must be made. Such was the case when I decided it was time to hang up my hospitality hat. Nothing specifically happened to get me to that point. For quite some time, I started to feel listless and unfulfilled. The career I'd always dreamed of evolved into just another job I felt obliged to show up to. The zest disappeared. The routine-ness of it made me feel hollow inside. As guests began to get ruder and more distasteful, I was unsure if I could continue to bite my tongue at the racist remarks, the unwarranted insults, and unconscionable demands hurled at me and the staff.

The gnawing in my gut that the inevitable end of this era would soon arrive, began the year my family endured the painstaking horror of watching my mother-in-law valiantly battle cancer. She ultimately died one August morning at the hospital, in my husband's arms. In an instant, our outlook on life shifted. The future would be different.

We understood, in that moment in time, that life was fleeting and uncertain. Goals we'd aspired to reach and glass ceilings we'd wanted to shatter, professionally, just didn't matter as much. Happiness and holistic health became paramount priorities. With my husband still reeling with despair and my children being shellshocked by the loss of their grandmother, I felt it was my duty to be my family's rock. On one hand, I found myself wanting to explore other avenues such as freelance journalism, photography, or consulting. On the other hand, all I wanted to do was be a wife and mom and slowly take a more active role in my family's business.

I'd enjoyed a stellar career up until that point, and was proud of all that I'd accomplished: the awards, the friendships, the life-changing experiences, traveling around the world, and the countless blessings. Most of all I was proud of the fact that I'd stayed true to myself. In an industry that could chew you up and spit you out if you let it, I ended my career on an authentic note just as I'd started it: I was still Jeannine, just a gal from St. Croix, U.S. Virgin Islands, who dreamed of having an illustrious career in tourism and hospitality since childhood. And I did.

After deciding I would step away from the industry I'd loved, I had only one new destination in mind: the state of Zen. As of now, I'm in this place. I think I'll stay here a while. And who knows? Maybe...just maybe...the hospitality itch will return. I'll just have to wait and see.

BONUS ALERT
Extra, Extra ... Read All About It!

There were so many other stories I thought to share. Some were just too gross; others could probably get me sued...or worse! However, there were some experiences that broke my heart or melted it in different ways. Too short for an entire dedicated chapter, here is some noteworthy bonus content...

VIRGIN TERRITORY

Nowadays, not too many brides walk down the aisle in white as display of purity. That's not me being judgmental, it's just a fact. And while this may be true, there are some anomalies. Such was the case with an outspoken, and, definitely blushing, new bride who hailed from South Carolina.

A genuine and shining example of "good Christian folks", Keira and her new husband descended upon our hotel in true wedded bliss. Giddy with joy at being in the islands for the first time, their adorable antics made the staff grin and blush right along with them. The southern belle and I had developed a great rapport during the three months prior to arrival. I'd arranged the couple's hiking excursions, private beach dinners, poolside couple massages and more. The carefully crafted itinerary was perfect. But in the words of John Lennon, "Life is what happens to you while you're busy making other plans."

The second morning after arrival, my newest newlywed girlfriend walked into my office and casually sat atop my desk. Amused at this action, but not upset, I asked her how the honeymoon was going. Her response was so blunt, I literally spit out my coffee. She asked me to get a very specific item for her if I could find it. Hilarious for me, but also deeply personal for her, I was equally honored and shocked she trusted me with the task. I nodded, as she spoke in a very serious demeanor, and told her I'd take care of her special request.

I was on shift alone for the next two hours, so I couldn't leave the property, but one hour and a few phone calls later, a familiar car rolled up to our hotel's main entrance. I walked out to it and grabbed a small brown paper bag from the driver. Asking how much was needed as reimbursement for the stuff in the bag, my dependable pal just waved me away with a laugh and started to drive from the property, slyly saying in that lilting Caribbean accent, "For sure, that gonna help your guest. I hear it does work wonders and get tings going in the right direction."

I peeked into the crumpled paper bag, noting it was exactly what Keira had asked for. I went back into my office and called her room to let her know her "saving grace" had arrived. Forty-five minutes later, she was back in my office, neon green beach bag over her shoulder. She gave me a big hug after she peeked into the brown paper bag that I handed to her. I didn't know what else to do except to ask, "Are you set? Do you need anything else? I'd be happy to run to the store before my shift ends."

She gave me that bright smile and, quickly stuffing the little paper bag into her bright beach bag, she said, "I think I'm good. Instructions are on it, right? Who knew losing my virginity would hurt so darn much? The past few nights have NOT been fun. But I'll figure it out. Hopefully, this KY Jelly does the trick. I'll let ya know. Thanks!"

With that, she left my office with a spring in her step and bold determination in her eyes. Her adoring and quiet hubby was in serious trouble! I knew I'd hear about that night's escapades the next day. And boy, oh boy, did I. Today, the lovely couple has four children and are headed to their 12th anniversary. Guess she figured it out after all!

DEMONS AMONG US

Over the years, many of the memories of my hospitality career have given me a reason to reflect with a smile or a snicker. A few of them make my blood boil. This is a story definitely falls into the "horrors" category. I guarantee it.

Dr. and Dr. Patel arrived with their two young children and their nanny. The smiling nanny, who looked to be in her late 50s, was a radiant Indian beauty. She carried most of the children's luggage and heavy backpacks on arrival. The staff quickly assisted her and took the excess items away from her so she could relax a bit. The Cross-Fit-addicted couple (by their own admission) had rented a 1200 square foot one-bedroom pool suite with a pull-out sofa plus two additional twin beds. They had been offered the two-bedroom suite, but even at a reduced rate for the upgrade, they refused. The typical arrival protocols followed, and the family was left to settle in and enjoy their first night.

The next afternoon, some of the housekeepers excitedly told me that the nanny, Nirmala, was from Guyana, where quite a few of the staff members—and most of my husband's family—hailed from as well. She had told some of the ladies that she'd left Guyana as a renowned seamstress and moved to New York. Unable to find a job, a friend suggested she apply to become a babysitter. That process led her to becoming the nanny of the family she now worked with.

I decided that we would make Nirmala feel extra special while in our care. I had heard that she was sleeping on the pull-out sofa and decided to upgrade the Patels to the two-bedroom suite, free of charge. We wanted to give our new Guyanese "aunty" a little something to smile about even though she was technically working and not on vacation.

Over the next few hours, the housekeepers transformed the formerly locked room. Almost as big as her employers' master bedroom, the staff easily fit the twin beds into the second suite. (Apparently, the Mr. and Mrs. were never to be disturbed at night by their 3- and 6-year-old children.) To finish off the kind gesture, we added some Guyanese treats like ICEE soda, mithai, and

salara. When we surprised Nirmala with her own luxury suite, her tear-filled eyes shone with palpable, con-
tagious joy. She only managed to stammer out a quiet
"thank you, thank you". Our team collectively felt like
Christmas morning came early and the gift we received
was seeing someone else be that happy and grateful. We
left her alone to enjoy her one and only day off, as the
family of four were on a tour of the island by boat with
lunch on a private cay.

The next morning, I stepped into my office with a bounce
in my step. I couldn't wait to hear how Nirmala had enjoyed her day off. Instead, a few minutes later, an irate
Mrs. Patel showed up knocking on my slightly ajar door.
With her rigid posture, the petite woman stood before
me in her all but 5'2" glory, looking pissed. I greeted her
and beckoned her to come in and have a seat. She didn't
wait for me to ask her what was wrong. In a no-nonsense manner, she said, "Nirmala can't have that room.
Please lock it and put things back the way they were." I
assumed she thought we would still charge her for the
second room, thus her attitude. I stressed to her that the
upgrade was complimentary, and no charges would be
billed.

She vehemently shook her head and through clenched
teeth, repeated, "I want Nirmala out of that room and
back on the couch in OUR suite. She is not supposed to
have that room. I'm paying for this vacation, and I probably pay your salary with what we've spent to be here.
Do as I say...NOW!" She immediately stood up and quite
literally marched out of my office. I sat there perplexed
as hell. I was also happy she'd left so abruptly because
the words that sat bubbling on the tip of my tongue were
about to be anything but professional.

A few minutes later, two of our housekeepers came to see me. I could see by the traumatized look on their faces, something had happened with the Patels. The story they told made me furious. I slammed my hand on my desk so hard, I almost broke my wrist.

The scenario went a little something like this: Dr. Patel (Mrs.) took a look at Nirmala's suite and said nothing. She quietly turned, ran into her own room, and grabbed Dr. Patel (Mr.) by his shirt and dragged him to see the nanny's room. The staff was refreshing it at the time, and overheard every bitter word that Mrs. P. screamed.

She griped, "This is too good for her, Raj. I don't want her getting spoiled. She works for us! She is NOT our equal and I will not tolerate this! Tell these idiots to get her out of this room and back on the sofa where she belongs. I can't have my kids thinking the help is special. She is the HELP! I'm going to the manager and find out who authorized this!" And Mr. Patel wholeheartedly nodded in agreement as he checked out the suite. I assume that was when the demon-witch ended up in my office.

After they finished telling me about the incident, I simultaneously wept and cursed. If this kind and sweet woman could be subjected to such treatment in front of strangers, I wondered how she was treated behind closed doors in New York. Heartbroken and numb, we did as Mrs. Patel asked.

Nirmala wasn't allowed to communicate with the staff after that day. In true 007 style, however, we "smuggled" some souvenirs and a hefty monetary gift to her the night before she left. To this day, I think about Nirmala and her rotten-to-the-core bosses. I pray she is in a much better situation today and happy.

ACKNOWLEDGMENTS

Grateful, thankful, blessed... it's the only way to describe how I feel right now. The desire to write a book has been burning inside of me since I was a girl attending elementary school. I wrote my first two books in my 40's as a testament to the fact that it is never too late to do something that you **REALLY** want to do. I thank God for allowing me the joy of seeing this dream come true.

Beyond thankful to my mother who has been my rock from day one. It's my turn to be your rock, Mom, and I will not fail or falter. You and Joselle are set!

To the three most important men in my life—my husband and my sons—I **LOVE YOU**. Without you, there is no me. I am blessed beyond measure to have you by my side, cheering me on when I feel deflated and overwhelmed. Your love means everything!

I could not have gotten here without the help of a phenomenal team of ladies. A heartfelt **THANK YOU** goes out to the kind and ever-so-brilliant Lil Barcaski and her team at GWN Publishing / Virtual Creatives, the amazing Kristina Conatser, Creative Design Director at Capturedbykcdesigns.com, and the multitalented Katelyn M. Stewart. If you dream of writing a book, trust me, these angels will make it happen!

To everyone who bought my debut books, you have my eternal gratitude. For every person who not only bought the book, but read it, left a great review, shared the book on your personal social media channels, shared my social media posts, or told someone else about my labor of love, **THANK YOU.**

I am thankful for the places that have helped to shape my life: St. Croix, St. Thomas, Anguilla, St. Maarten/St. Martin, Cayman Islands, and Florida. Visit these places when you can and be sure to take a copy of my books with you!

TO ALL MY FRIENDS AND FAMILY, thank you for your support, encouragement, prayers and unending love. I did it, y'all! **ONE LOVE!**

JEANNINE CONNOR GITTENS was born and raised on St. Croix, US Virgin Islands to Anguillian parents. She is a small business owner, Realtor, Spanish teacher, 80's music fanatic, hodophile and self-certified "beach bum." Having enjoyed a successful career in hospitality spanning many zip codes and area codes, her adopted motto of, "Love All, Serve All," rings true in all she does. She spends her time between her homes in the Caribbean and Florida, and prefers to *"catch flights, not feelings."*